T0169286

asterisk

asterisk

poems

Jenny George

BULL★CITY
PRESS
Durham, NC

Library of Congress Cataloging-in-Publication Data

Names: George, Jenny, author.
Title: Asterisk : poems / Jenny George.
Description: Durham, NC : Bull City Press, 2023.
Identifiers: LCCN 2023027952 |
ISBN 9781949344493 (softcover)
Subjects: LCGFT: Poetry.
Classification: LCC PS3607.E66295 A93 2023 |
DDC 811/.6--dc23/eng/20230629
LC record available at https://lccn.loc.gov/2023027952

Published in the United States of America

Cover image by Eli Afram
Book design by Spock and Associates

Published by BULL CITY PRESS
1217 Odyssey Drive
Durham, NC 27713

www.BullCityPress.com

Contents

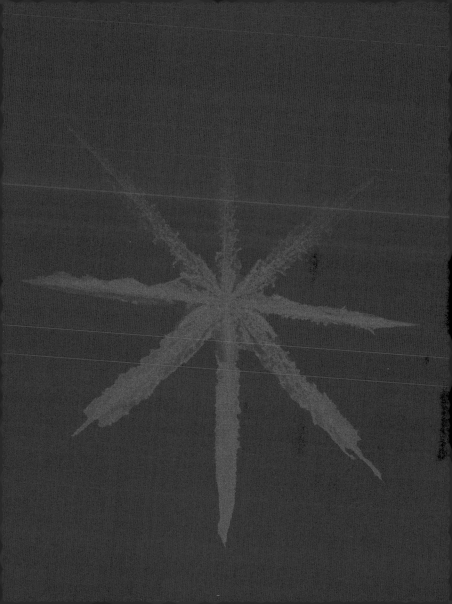

*

You become Not-you.
A postcard of snow.
They tell me you
are at "rest."
In the window's cold
rectangle: a rose arbor
shipwrecked in a white field.

Snowstorm, April 28

You were not dead.
How could you be
when never once
before in all this
time had you
been other than
alive, and famously?
A fury of snow.
You were not dead.
The air a world
of cold white bees.

Anniversary

Abruptly awake. The room
moon-occupied, unfamiliar.
Whatever *it* is, it can disappear.

Over time the sun seeps in,
an opened yolk.

Now the birds are our marriage.
I put the seeds out
every morning
on a white plate.

7 lbs. 14 oz.

They burned you down to a box
and gave you back
to me like that—newborn dust,
your exact birthweight's
worth—now wrapped in a black
velvet bag and delivered
into my remaining hands.

Orpheus in the Garden

I'm on my knees again
planting hard peas
like a row of tiny brains.
I drive each one deep
into the cold obstruction.

A Grammar

She passed.
Passed on; passed over.
She's past. She is in
the past now.
In other words
she is not
here.
But these lilacs shivering
in a spring
profusion:
Her and her and her.
I bury my
face in them.

Last Swim

Beneath our joy
big catfish rested
in the lake's pockets,
fish the color
of the lake, invisible
until we saw
the dark shapes move.

3 a.m.

Half-awake, you draw back in
the hand
that hangs over the abyss:

The Lions

You can't take them with you,
they said to you at the crossing.
You can't
take anything.

Now I have your lions.

At night I feel the warm breaths
venting off them.
A large stillness watches me
from the alien rooms of their eyes.
When I walk into the orchard
they follow me as far as the trees.

Abandon the Usual Instruments

To want nothing: you thought
it was freedom. Then the body
was removed.
A wind in the apple grove.
Wind that doubles the grove—marrying it,
marrying it—like a hand
touching her dresses, those replicas
hung in the closet.

Memory

Looking up at me from her bath
she said, *Remember
everything we ever did?* A garland
of bones down her back.

Egg

There is only dark.
Then, a crack.
The crack defines the dark. It makes
an edge. A start.
Like how we only know we *sleep*
at the point sleep breaks.
From that place
of part-wake
we recognize the depths.
And now the hard life waits.

Midwinter

The window's toothed with icicles.
A large cold rings out.
Belowground the ants
are frozen dewdrops of armor
waiting for their mania to be restored.
You light the stove, put the kettle on.
Silence is healed over. A cosmos
of miniscule stars throbs inside the earth.

As a Daffodil

I broke my paper clothes.
I used the cold
and made a vacancy:
a breathing out. The door
of the world stood open.
I readied Myself.

About the Title

A figure used to indicate omission, endnote, reference, et cetera, or to distinguish phrases as conjectural. Late 14th century, from the Greek *asteriskos,* "little star."

Acknowledgments

Poems in this book have appeared in *The Poetry Review UK* and *Sixth Finch*.

Gratitude to the editors of those journals.

About the Author

Jenny George is the author of *The Dream of Reason* (Copper Canyon Press, 2018). She lives in Santa Fe, New Mexico.

Also by Jenny George

The Dream of Reason